ALL THE BEST PASTA SAUCES II

Cookbooks by Joie Warner
ALL THE BEST PASTA SAUCES
ALL THE BEST SALADS
ALL THE BEST PIZZAS
ALL THE BEST CHICKEN DINNERS
ALL THE BEST MEXICAN MEALS
ALL THE BEST MUFFINS AND QUICK BREADS
ALL THE BEST POTATOES
ALL THE BEST COOKIES
ALL THE BEST PASTA SAUCES II
ALL THE BEST RICE
THE COMPLETE BOOK OF CHICKEN WINGS
THE BRAUN HAND BLENDER COOKBOOK
A TASTE OF CHINATOWN
JOIE WARNER'S SPAGHETTI
JOIE WARNER'S CAESAR SALADS
JOIE WARNER'S APPLE DESERTS

ALL THE BEST

PASTA SAUCES II

BY
JOIE WARNER

HEARST BOOKS • New York

LIBRARY OF CONGRESS CATALOGING-IN-PUBLICATION DATA
Warner, Joie.
    All the best pasta sauces II/by Joie Warner.
        p.   cm.
Includes index.
ISBN 0-688-13348-7
1. Sauces.   2. Cookery (Pasta)   I. Title.   II. Title: All the best pasta sauces two.   III. Title: Pasta Sauces II.
TX819.A1W372   1994
641.8'22 -- dc20   94-20764
                                                              CIP

Printed in the United States of America
10 9 8 7 6 5 4 3 2 1

This book was created and produced by

Flavor Publications, Inc.
208 East 51st Street, Suite 240
New York, New York 10022

ACKNOWLEDGMENTS

THANKS TO Sarah Best, Susan Allen, Debbie Fine, Amy Lee, Maura Segal, Louise and Thom Northrop, Paul Paganelli, Sharee Fiore, Kathleen Johnson, Annie Hogan, Marcia Lowther, Susan Grant, and Margaret Jackson.

tomato

CONTENTS

INTRODUCTION

My passion for pasta continues unabated: I never seem to run out of ideas for different combinations and permutations of ingredients, or new pasta pairings to try. And it's gratifying to discover that there are thousands of pasta lovers out there, too, who are so enamored of pasta's incredible versatility, wholesomeness, affordability, and ease of preparation that they clamored for this sequel to my earlier book *All the Best Pasta Sauces*.

It really is hard to believe that just a few years ago pasta was simply seen as a cheap-and-cheerful standby, useful when time – and especially money – was tight. Then it became an overnight sensation – the rage of the '80s – and the most sought-after (and ridiculously expensive) choice in restaurants and cafés. We now have designer pasta in all shapes, colors, textures and sizes, and it seems there's a fresh pasta shop popping up on every street corner in every town.

Incredibly, pasta's whirlwind celebrity had some people thinking it was just a passing fad. But how could something so quick to cook, so healthful, and so utterly delicious not become one of our most important foods? If anything, pasta is so well established, it's now as American as apple pie!

Today, many of us are preparing this wholesome staple several times a week for easy, speedy suppers; as light lunches; and as the focal point of dazzling dinners. But it wasn't so long ago that pasta, like potatoes, had a bad name in some quarters for the company it sometimes ran with. It's true that some of those cream- and cheese-laden sauces are a little heavy on the old cholesterol. But it's easy to avoid, or to take very small servings of those rich sauces if you are concerned about saturated fats in your diet. Instead, make your sauces with plenty of good-for-you vegetables and extra-virgin olive oil, which has been shown to actually reduce cholesterol levels. Add garlic to your heart's content, for studies have shown it helps prevent a number of diseases – including cancer. Serve it up with a glass of red wine (I always knew the French were onto something), and you have one of the most salubrious meals going.

In this second pasta book, the recipes are organized by type of sauce, with recommendations as to what pasta goes best. You'll find chapters on Uncooked Pasta Sauces, Cheese and Butter Sauces, Tomato Sauces, Vegetable and Bean Sauces, Seafood and Fish Sauces, and Meat Sauces. The recipes range from the classic to the exotic and in this eclectic collection of over sixty totally new recipes you'll find a pasta sauce for every occasion and every taste. In keeping with my philosophy – the quicker the ingredients are cooked, the fresher, healthier, and more flavorful the outcome – you'll find that very few take longer to prepare than the pasta takes to cook. In fact, many sauces require no cooking at all – how's that for simple?

My emphasis is on garden-fresh produce and herbs, though there are a few sensuous butter-and-cream sauces that will satisfy the soul of the most sybaritic. I've devised the majority of the following recipes using good-for-you olive oil. To lighten them even more, you may use a little less oil than I've suggested (but remember to reduce the amount of Parmesan cheese in recipes where it's added to the sauce, or the pasta will be dry). Or you may substitute an equal amount of pasta cooking water (added when tossing the pasta and sauce together) for some of the olive oil. In a few recipes, I add a bit of butter at the end of cooking for added richness, but you may leave it out if you wish (but I hope you won't!). After all, once my recipes come into your kitchen, you are free to adapt them to your own particular lifestyle and make them your own.

What I love most about pasta is that it's so effortless to turn even the simplest ingredients found in the pantry – a few tablespoons of olive oil and a sprinkling of Parmesan, or some fresh parsley and tins of tomatoes and tuna – into a totally satisfying pasta sauce.

My pantry always holds a wide selection of dried pasta shapes – spaghetti, linguine, gnocchi (dried – not the fresh variety), conchiglie, penne, rigatoni, fusilli, farfalle, and macaroni. I'm never without a bottle of good olive oil; lots of fresh garlic and onions (red, white, yellow); a couple of pint baskets of cherry or plum tomatoes; plenty of dried herbs and spices; several cans of tomatoes, chickpeas, and cannellini beans; tins of tuna, anchovies, and sardines, as well as jars of roasted red peppers, bottled hot pepper rings, capers, pickled jalapeños, marinated artichokes, plus a bottle of balsamic vinegar and a dry white vermouth. My refrigerator is stocked with sun-dried tomatoes in oil, Kalamata olives, fresh basil, parsley, mint, lemons, limes, oranges, sweet peppers, mushrooms, green onions, and other fresh vegetables of many kinds. There's also hefty chunks of Parmesan and Romano cheeses, wedges of Gorgonzola and Brie, and sliced pancetta and prosciutto. My freezer contains sweet and hot Italian sausage, ground beef, and frozen vegetables such as peas, lima beans, and corn. Even with only a few of these pantry staples on hand you're guaranteed to have the makings of a terrific spur-of-the-moment family meal or an impromptu dinner for unexpected guests. Add a bottle of wine, a crisp green salad, and some country bread, and your spontaneous pasta repast is transformed into a fabulous feast.

A friend of mine said recently, "pasta is such a smart choice for a healthy diet and is so loved by everybody – kids and adults alike – you can never have too many recipes!" I do hope you will add my new pasta recipes to your repertoire of favorites, and I wish you as much joy and pleasure in trying these pasta sauces for yourself as I had in their creation.

JOIE WARNER

◆ ◆ ◆

B ASIC S

H OW AND WHAT TO BUY

Quality is the key when buying pasta. While all the many different brands may look the same, they certainly don't taste the same. And then there's the debate over dried versus fresh pasta. Contrary to what many would have you believe, fresh pasta is not superior to dried and I think both are equally delicious. To add to the confusion,,both dried and fresh pasta come in countless varieties. Now, while each variety has its own taste and texture and is often paired with a specific sauce, there's really no great mystery to it at all as you'll see as I divulge the secrets to successful pasta dishes.

Here are some pointers to help you find your way through what at first seems like a plethora of pasta.

ITALIAN AND DOMESTIC DRIED PASTA: The best dried pasta is made from water mixed with durum (hard) wheat that has been ground into semolina. All Italian dried pasta and most American brands are made with this preferred wheat, which contains more proteins and vitamins than does regular flour. The dough is mixed, kneaded, stretched, and extruded or stamped out to form the desired shape, then dried. Spaghetti, macaroni, and rigatoni are the most familiar pastas in this category. Some American manufacturers use a combination of semolina and common flours to produce a pasta that is acceptable when cooked properly, but which is very easily overcooked as it takes less time than that made with just semolina. Pasta made with 100% durum semolina takes a few minutes longer to cook but it is more resilient. Good pasta has a subtle, nutty taste and a chewy texture all its own. That is why, in Italy, pasta is appreciated in its own right and not seen simply as a vehicle for the sauce.

Supermarkets carry a good selection of both domestic and imported dried pastas, or you can find a wide variety of imported brands in Italian grocery stores or specialty food stores. Dried pasta can be stored in a cool, dry cupboard almost indefinitely in its unopened package or in a sealed container.

There are over 100 names for the wide variety of shapes, sizes, thicknesses, and textures of Italian dried pastas and, to make matters worse, the names change from region to region. To help sort them out, here's a chart of the most commonly found dried pasta varieties.

SPECIALTY PASTA: Other dried varieties are made from Jerusalem artichoke flour, buckwheat flour, soy flour (high in protein), and whole wheat flour. They can usually be found in health food stores and some supermarkets and they have a unique taste and texture all their own.

ASIAN AND EUROPEAN NOODLES: Asian noodles are made from a variety of wheat flours, vegetable starches, and rice flours. Wheat flour noodles (non-egg and egg noodles) are sold fresh or frozen in plastic bags (chow mein is the most familiar). Vegetable starch noodles (mung bean or cellophane noodles) are usually sold dried in clear cellophane packages. Rice flour noodles (rice stick or rice vermicelli and fresh rice noodles) are sold both fresh and dried. Buckwheat noodles (soba) are sold dried in clear plastic packages. These noodles are available at Asian food stores and some health food stores.

FRESH PASTA: Freshly made or home-made pasta is softer and more delicately flavored than dried. High in moisture, it cooks very quickly and weighs more than dried pasta. You therefore need to add a little more than the quantities shown in the recipes.

Shops that make fresh pasta on-site are popping up all over the place and many supermarkets carry fresh pastas, which need refrigeration and must be eaten soon after purchasing. Some fresh pastas take as little as a half-minute to cook. And, of course, you can make your own.

Fresh noodles can be prepared with all-purpose flour, eggs, salt and no water; with all-purpose flour, water, and salt; or with a mixture of finely milled durum wheat, all-purpose flour, and water. You can do all the steps by hand or you can use a food

capellini
spaghettini
spaghetti
linguine
fettuccine
ziti
cut ziti
fusilli
rotelle
penne rigate
farfalline
farfalle
orecchiette
gnocchi
rigatoni
conchiglie

d r i e d   p a s t a

processor and a manual pasta machine. If you do want to make it yourself, there are excellent recipes in *The Classic Italian Cookbook*, by Marcella Hazan, and *The Fine Art of Italian Cooking*, by Giuliano Bugialli.

Ingredients are sometimes added to make beautifully colored pastas – tomatoes or carrots for orange, spinach for green, beets for red, cocoa for brown, squid's ink for black – or you can add herbs to the dough to delicately enhance the taste.

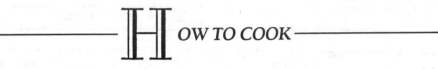

HOW TO COOK

Pasta is one of the simplest foods to cook, yet one of the easiest to spoil by over-cooking.

For up to 1 pound of pasta, bring 4 to 5 quarts of water to a furious boil. The strands will stick together if the pasta is not cooked in enough liquid. Just before adding the pasta, stir in 1 to 2 tablespoons salt, if desired. Do not add oil. Add pasta to the boiling water all at once (spaghetti and other long pastas should be pushed down with a wooden spoon until completely submerged – never broken into smaller pieces) and immediately begin stirring with a wooden spoon. Cover the pot briefly to bring water quickly back to a boil, then remove cover or it will boil over. Stir again to separate strands and place lid halfway on to maintain a rapid boil. Remove cover occasionally and stir until pasta is *al dente*, which means the pasta is completely tender but still firm and chewy. Be careful, too, not to undercook the pasta or it will be completely inedible.

Dried pasta can take several minutes to cook, but start testing for doneness after a few minutes when the pasta has become limp. Test by biting into a piece. Do not rely on package instructions: they invariably show times that are much too long. Keep testing every few minutes until the white core has almost disappeared and the texture is to your taste.

Fresh, home-made noodles take only seconds to cook; store-bought fresh noodles will take 1 to 2 minutes.

The moment the pasta is done, drain it in a colander. Do not rinse the pasta unless the recipe says so or the sauce will not cling. Shake the colander to remove excess water (especially important with tubular and shell-shaped pastas), but don't overdo it – a little moisture is necessary or the resulting dish could turn out dry. Toss the pasta immediately with the sauce or it will continue cooking and stick together.

Some cooks add a little olive oil or butter to the drained pasta to prevent the strands from sticking, but this is not necessary unless the recipe so specifies.

QUANTITIES

It is difficult to give the exact number of servings for pasta because there are so many variables. In Italy, 4 ounces of dried pasta per serving is the rule, although Italians do not typically eat pasta as a main course as do we Americans. I find 4 ounces per person is about right for a main dish serving of the long, thin pastas, such as spaghetti, and this amount works well for side dishes and first courses, too. For heartier pastas such as penne or rigatoni, I measure ½ pound for 2 servings and ¾ pound for 4 servings. If the sauce is substantial or rich, ½ pound of pasta will yield 4 servings and ¾ pound may yield up to 6 servings. You'll need to adjust the quantities to suit the appetites of your family and friends. I use a kitchen scale to weigh my pasta, but it's easy to divide each 1-pound package into quarters and go from there.

When using fresh pasta, add 1½ ounces more per ¾-pound serving, or 2 ounces more for a 1-pound serving.

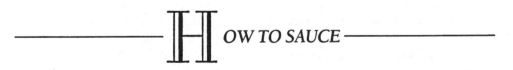

HOW TO SAUCE

I'm sure you, too, have noticed that we are adding less sauce these days as we learn to appreciate the taste of the pasta itself and, as we become more health conscious, the sauces themselves are also much lighter.

There are really only two rules: don't overcook the sauce and don't over-sauce the pasta. The sauce should gently coat the pasta, not drown it! My proportion of sauce to pasta may be a little more generous than the Italians recommend, and some cooks may want to add another 2 ounces of pasta to my recommended amount.

Limited only by our imagination, there are sauces for every shape of pasta, for every taste, and for every day of the week. In fact, I've heard it said that in

Italy you could have a different sauce every day of the year.

Sauces range from the quick-and-easy olive oil and Parmesan, to the more complex variety, but none takes very long to prepare. Feel free to mix and match sauces to the different types of pasta: just bear in mind that there are a few basic, but flexible (Italians tend to be more strict) rules.

The different shapes, sizes, and surfaces have different qualities designed for different sauces and ingredients. Long, thin varieties, such as spaghetti, linguine, and capellini, generally go well with uncooked or light sauces based on tomatoes, vegetables, seafood, or olive oil (for example, pesto, clam, garlic and oil). Long, flat shapes like fresh fettucine match wonderfully well with a light cream or cheese sauce. Thick, tubular shapes – penne, rigatoni – pair well with meat and vegetable sauces. Shell-shaped conchiglie and lumache, and cup shapes like orecchiette, go best with small bits of vegetables, meat, and fish in a slightly soupy sauce that can be caught up in the hollows. Fusilli or rotelle – any of the twisted or wheel varieties – catch small bits in their whorls and spirals, so they go with sauces that are neither too thick nor too chunky, while pappardelle, a wide, fresh ribbon pasta, is famous served with rabbit sauce, although it can be matched with other assertive meat sauces.

By the way, these mixing and matching rules do not apply to Asian noodles since they come in only one shape – long and skinny. Instead, in Asian cuisines, noodles are matched with the cooking technique: fried fresh noodles (chow mein), deep-fried or braised bean thread noodles, or hot or cold sauced buckwheat noodles.

So, while you can match just about any sauce to any pasta, it is wise to substitute a pasta that is similar in shape and texture to that recommended in the recipe.

Cooking times are given, but there are so many variables that it's hard to be exact. Basically, the sauce should cling nicely to the pasta. It should not be too thick and heavy – that's guaranteed to turn the pasta into a gluey mess – nor too thin to coat. Err on the under– rather than over-cooked side: you can always put the pasta – sauce and all – back into the skillet and stir over low heat until properly thickened. But an overcooked sauce will ruin the pasta, too.

And remember that old Italian saying: "Guests must wait for the pasta, pasta never waits for the guests." The sauce must be ready the instant the pasta is drained. I prepare my sauce while the pasta is boiling, or I cook it first and have it ready with the element turned off. When the pasta reaches the *al dente* stage, I turn the heat back on to gently reheat the sauce while I drain the pasta. Then I quickly toss the two together and serve up immediately.

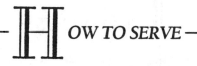OW TO SERVE

Once the pasta is drained, immediately add it to the sauce in the skillet (or put the drained pasta in a serving bowl and pour the sauce over the pasta). Next, toss gently with two forks and transfer to a warmed, wide, shallow serving bowl or individual heated plates. Pasta purists never use metal tools for tossing or serving: they use specially designed wooden spoons or forks. But I find that metal dinner forks do just fine.

To serve long, thin strands, lift a small portion of pasta well up over the serving dish and then place it on heated plates or in wide bowls. Don't forget a large serving spoon to scoop out the ingredients that are always hiding at the bottom of the serving dish!

Special pasta serving bowls can be found in most kitchen specialty shops, along with the wide, rather shallow bowls that are traditionally used for individual pasta servings because they help keep the pasta warm longer, hold the sauce and pasta together – and the sides make it easier to twirl the pasta around your fork. Don't forget to warm the dishes: pasta cools off fast.

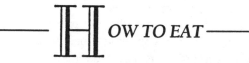OW TO EAT

The short answer is – with gusto – and without a lot of fuss about being neat and tidy!

Italians and Asians think it's just fine to noisily slurp their noodles, and I heartily agree with them. The Chinese and Japanese use chopsticks to transfer strands to their mouths and then they literally suck in the noodles – just like your kids do when you're not looking.

Here's the correct way to do it. First, gather a few long strands between the tines of your fork and twirl them around a couple of times until a bundle forms with a few strands dangling. You may place the tip of the fork against the plate edge or sides of the bowl to assist in the twirling process. Some use a large spoon as a base to twirl their pasta but this is not correct – and considered gauche: the spoon is meant for scooping the sauce that remains in the bottom of the bowl.

INGREDIENTS

ANCHOVIES: My recipes use the canned anchovy fillets in oil.

BLACK OLIVES: I use Kalamata olives from Greece. You may also use Niçoise olives from France. Both are available in supermarket delis or specialty food shops. Canned American olives do not have the flavor or pungency needed for these recipes.

BLACK PEPPER: I always use freshly ground black peppercorns. When I suggest "lots of freshly ground black pepper," I mean at least 10 grindings of the pepper mill. In addition, most sauces need a few extra grindings of pepper at the table.

CANNELLINI: These are Italian white kidney beans that are available dried or canned. The recipes in this book use the canned variety.

CAPERS: These are the unopened flower buds of a Mediterranean shrub. Many cooks prefer the tiny French capers but I generally use the large variety in my pasta sauces because they have a stronger flavor. They are packed in vinegar (not salt), and I never rinse them.

CHILES: The recipes you will find here call for the readily available – and more convenient – pickled sliced chiles (see Jalapeños).

CILANTRO: A pungent herb also known as coriander or Chinese parsley.

CREMINI MUSHROOMS: These are brown-skinned mushrooms that are available in many supermarkets and specialty food stores.

DRIED HERBS: The fresher the dried herbs, the more flavorful your cooking. To release their flavor, crumble them in your fingers before adding them to the sauce. If they have lost their color and aroma, it is best to replace them.

ESCAROLE: A frizzy-leafed, slightly bitter-tasting lettuce with leaves that are pale green at the top and yellowish-white at the bottom.

FETA CHEESE: A slightly firm, white cheese, originally from Greece. It is available in many supermarkets, specialty cheese shops, and Greek food markets.

FRESH HERBS: Do not substitute dried herbs if fresh are called for in a recipe.

GARLIC: It is hard to imagine anyone not cooking with garlic (lots!), for it is a seasoning that goes with almost every savory dish. Choose large bulbs that are tightly closed and not sprouting. Squeeze the bulb to make sure it is firm and fresh. Avoid powdered garlic.

GENOA SAUSAGE: An Italian cured sausage you will find in the deli counter at the supermarket, Italian food markets, or at specialty food stores.

GORGONZOLA: A very creamy, mold-ripened cheese from the Lombardy region of

Italy. Its sharp flavor is wonderful in cream sauces. It is available in Italian food markets, well-stocked cheese stores, and some supermarkets.

HOT PEPPER RINGS: Bottled pickled sliced red and yellow hot peppers are available in supermarkets. They are typically used on pizzas and in sandwiches and salads.

JALAPEÑOS: I use the readily available jars of pickled and sliced chiles. They are available in supermarkets in the Mexican food section.

MEZITHRA: A hard, Greek cheese with a distinctive taste; look for it at Greek food markets and well-stocked cheese shops.

OLIVE OIL: I prefer using an extra-virgin olive oil with a delicate olive taste.

PANCETTA: An unsmoked Italian-style bacon that is seasoned with pepper and spices, then rolled. It is found mainly at Italian food markets and some supermarkets.

PARMESAN: Be sure to purchase Parmesan that has the words "Parmigiano Reggiano" or, second best, "Grana Padano" stamped on the rind. Always grate it fresh just before using because it begins to lose flavor after grating. It is available in Italian food markets or well-stocked cheese stores and keeps for several months.

PROSCIUTTO: This salted, air-dried Italian ham is available in Italian food shops and at some supermarket deli counters.

RICOTTA: Fresh ricotta resembles cottage cheese in that it is a soft, white curd cheese, but it is finer in taste and texture. They are not interchangeable. It is available in Italian food shops, well-stocked cheese stores, and at some supermarkets.

SALT: Fear of salt has prompted many cooks to abandon it, but without salt, your pasta sauces will taste flat. Unless you're on a salt-restricted diet, make sure you add enough to bring out the flavors of the ingredients.

SHALLOTS: These small, brown-skinned onions have a delicate onion-garlic flavor. If unavailable, I often substitute a little minced garlic and onion.

SUN-DRIED TOMATOES: These have become very popular in recent years. I use sun-dried tomatoes packed in olive oil in my recipes. They are available in most specialty and Italian food markets and at many supermarket deli counters. Avoid any that are brownish colored.

TOMATOES, CANNED: Buy the best domestic or Italian brands available (experiment until you find a brand you like), for it makes an enormous difference in the taste and quality of the sauce. Del Monte, Redpack, and Di Napoli are considered good brands by many food experts. Crush canned tomatoes with your hands as you add them to the sauce, or crush them in the skillet with a wooden spoon if you don't like getting your hands messy.

Tomatoes, Fresh: Use only flavorful, ripe, unwaxed tomatoes. I suggest cherry tomatoes in many of my recipes: they are available year round and are generally more flavorful than out-of-season tomatoes. I don't bother skinning or seeding them, but if you're bothered by seeds, then go ahead and de-seed. If unwaxed plum tomatoes are available, by all means use them in place of cherry tomatoes. Plum tomatoes have less juice and therefore needn't be drained when suggested in recipes but since they are easy to seed, they should be seeded. If tomatoes are not fully ripe when purchased, do not refrigerate, but allow them to ripen at room temperature.

Vermouth: I use French dry white vermouth in my recipes instead of dry white wine: it keeps well after opening.

Zest: The colored outer layer of skin on a citrus fruit.

EQUIPMENT

Colander: The larger, the better, it should have feet or a stand to hold it upright in the sink.

Cheese Grater: For grating Parmesan or other hard cheeses.

Food Processor: Great for grating hard cheeses and for puréeing sauces.

Heavy Skillets And Saucepans: Essential; flimsy skillets and saucepans are not recommended as food sticks and burns. I use a heavy, large nonreactive skillet (one that doesn't react with acid foods such as tomatoes and lemons) for making my pasta sauces.

Large Pot: You will need a pot that holds at least 5 quarts for cooking pasta.

Pasta Serving Bowls: These wide, shallow bowls, about 12 inches in diameter and 2½-inches deep, help retain the heat longer than a serving platter.

Peppermill: Essential for cooking and for the table.

Spaghetti Cooker: These large pots have a built-in strainer and although I have never used one, a lot of people I know swear by them.

Spaghetti Spoon Or Fork: These plastic or wooden pronged utensils are for lifting strands of spaghetti from the cooking pot or for tossing pasta with sauce. Most Italians prefer them but I find dinner forks work just as well.

Wooden Spoons: Better than metal spoons for stirring pasta or sauces.

Zester: A small tool that cuts fine strips from lemon and orange peel.

UNCOOKED

SAUCES

◆ ◆ ◆

J ust crazy for the flavor of lemon? Combine it with fragrant fresh basil, toss it with a tangle of angel hair pasta, and you've got a delicate dish that's made in a jiff.

Lemons

LEMON AND FRESH BASIL SAUCE

Grated zest of 2 medium lemons
2 tablespoons fresh lemon juice
¼ cup fresh basil leaves, shredded, plus extra for garnish
2 tablespoons freshly grated Parmesan cheese, plus extra for serving

3 tablespoons butter, at room temperature
Salt
Lots of freshly ground black pepper

PLACE LEMON ZEST, lemon juice, basil, cheese, butter, salt, and pepper in large serving bowl. Add drained hot pasta and toss until combined. Garnish with basil and serve with extra cheese. Serves 3 to 4.

Recommended Pasta: ½ pound capellini, vermicelli, or spaghetti

MINT PESTO SAUCE

2 large garlic cloves
½ cup lightly packed fresh
   mint leaves
½ cup lightly packed fresh
   flat-leaf parsley leaves
½ cup lightly packed fresh
   basil leaves
¼ cup shelled natural-
   colored pistachios

½ cup olive oil
½ cup freshly grated
   Parmesan cheese
Salt
Freshly ground black
   pepper
Grated zest of 1 medium
   lemon (optional)

CHOP GARLIC, mint, parsley, basil, and pistachios in food processor – not too finely. With machine running, drizzle in oil. Stir in cheese, salt, pepper, and lemon zest. Taste for seasoning. Toss ½ the pesto sauce with drained hot pasta in large serving bowl, adding more according to taste and amount of pasta – a little pesto goes a long way. Serves 4 to 6.

Recommended Pasta: ½ to 1 pound spaghetti, fettuccine, or tagliatelle

Fresh mint, parsley, and basil blended with pistachios offer a pleasing change of pace from traditional pesto. The mint is not a strong presence and the pistachios add a special color and crunch. ♦ But don't use nuts that have been tinted red – only the natural ones. ♦ To save left-over pesto, add just enough olive oil to completely cover the sauce. It will keep for up to a month.

Cherry tomatoes, pungent cilantro, sweet corn, and jalapeños make a terrifically tangy sauce to toss with al dente noodles. If you wish, you may omit the corn for a more traditional – and equally sassy – salsa.

TOMATO, CORN, AND CHILE SALSA

2 large garlic cloves
¼ cup coarsely chopped red onion
¼ cup pickled sliced jalapeños, drained, chopped
1 pound ripe cherry tomatoes
1 cup fresh or frozen corn kernels, cooked

¼ cup olive oil
½ teaspoon salt
Freshly ground black pepper
½ cup fresh cilantro leaves, chopped
Freshly grated Parmesan cheese

CHOP GARLIC in food processor. Add onion, chiles, and tomatoes and chop – do not purée. Transfer mixture to footed strainer and set in sink for 5 minutes to drain. Place mixture in large serving bowl and stir in corn, oil, salt, pepper, and cilantro. Add drained hot pasta and toss until combined. Serve with cheese if desired. Serves 2 to 4.

Recommended Pasta: ½ pound penne rigate or fusilli

TOMATO, BASIL, AND BRIE SAUCE

3 large garlic cloves
1 pound ripe cherry
  tomatoes
¾ pound Brie cheese, rind
  removed, cubed
½ cup fresh basil leaves,
  shredded

¼ cup olive oil
Salt
Freshly ground black
  pepper
Freshly grated Parmesan
  cheese

CHOP GARLIC in food processor. Add tomatoes and chop – do not purée. Transfer mixture to footed strainer and set in sink for 5 minutes to drain. Place in large serving bowl and stir in Brie, basil, oil, salt, and pepper. Add drained hot pasta and toss until combined. Serve at once with Parmesan cheese if desired. Serves 2 to 4.

Recommended Pasta: ½ pound spaghetti

B *rie adds a subtle, yet stylish note to this sublimely seductive sauce.* ◆ *It's easier to trim and cube the Brie when chilled, but bring to room temperature before tossing with the pasta.*

asy to make, smooth and luscious, with bits of basil and red tomato scattered throughout, this sauce also suits hearty pastas like penne or fusilli.

TOMATO RICOTTA SAUCE

½ cup ricotta cheese, at
   room temperature
¼ cup freshly grated
   Parmesan cheese
¼ cup (½ stick) butter,
   melted
2 large ripe plum tomatoes,
   seeded, chopped

1 tablespoon chopped fresh
   basil leaves
Salt
Freshly ground black
   pepper

COMBINE RICOTTA and Parmesan cheese, butter, tomatoes, basil, salt, and pepper in large serving bowl. Add drained hot pasta and toss until combined. Serves 2.

Recommended Pasta: 6 ounces spaghetti

LIME AND TOMATO SALSA

2 large garlic cloves	¼ cup fresh lime juice
1 pound ripe cherry tomatoes	1 tablespoon Tabasco
½ teaspoon salt	¼ cup olive oil
Freshly ground black pepper	¼ cup freshly grated Parmesan cheese, plus extra for serving
Grated zest of 1 large lime	

CHOP GARLIC in food processor. Add tomatoes and chop – do not purée. Transfer mixture to footed strainer and set in sink for 5 minutes to drain. Place in large serving bowl and stir in salt, pepper, lime zest, lime juice, Tabasco, oil, and cheese. Add drained hot pasta and toss until combined. Serve with extra cheese if desired. Serves 2 to 4.

Recommended Pasta: ½ pound penne rigate or spaghetti

H*ot and significantly citrusy. I laced tomato salsa with the zest of lime and plenty of Tabasco – and I love it!* But be warned: it's not for the faint of heart. ♦ The salsa must be freshly made, then immediately tossed with al dente pasta. ♦ Because the sauce is slightly soupy, I like to serve it in wide shallow pasta bowls.

L emon is probably not the first seasoning that springs to mind for enhancing tomatoes, but – believe it or not -- they are made for each other. Lemon lovers (like me) will adore this zippy sauce.

TOMATO-LEMON SAUCE

2 large garlic cloves
1 pound ripe cherry
  tomatoes
Grated zest of 2 medium
  lemons
½ teaspoon salt

Freshly ground black
  pepper
¼ cup olive oil
Freshly grated Parmesan
  cheese

CHOP GARLIC in food processor. Add tomatoes and chop – do not purée. Transfer mixture to footed strainer and set in sink for 5 minutes to drain. Place in large serving bowl and stir in lemon zest, salt, pepper, and oil. Add drained hot pasta and toss until combined. Serve with cheese. Serves 2 to 4.

Recommended Pasta: ½ pound fusilli, penne rigate, or spaghetti

UNCOOKED PUTTANESCA SAUCE

2 large garlic cloves,
  chopped
1 pound fresh ripe
  tomatoes, seeded,
  coarsely chopped
¼ cup olive oil
½ teaspoon dried basil
  or oregano
¼ teaspoon hot red
  pepper flakes
Salt
Freshly ground black
  pepper

10 Greek black olives
  (Kalamata), pitted, cut
  into strips
2 tablespoons large capers,
  drained
¼ cup fresh flat-leaf parsley,
  chopped
2 tablespoons freshly
  grated Parmesan cheese,
  plus extra for serving

COMBINE GARLIC, tomatoes, oil, basil, red pepper flakes, salt, pepper, olives, capers, parsley, and cheese in large serving bowl. Add drained hot pasta and toss until combined. Serve with extra cheese and pass the peppermill. Serves 2 to 4.

Recommended Pasta: ½ pound penne rigate or spaghetti

ecause I received so many letters from readers who loved my rambunctious rendition of lusty Puttanesca sauce, I was inspired to devise an uncooked version. It's fresh and fabulous – I know you'll relish it this way, too! ◆ *Full-flavored tomatoes are essential.*

P antry pasta: sardines from the cupboard, lemons and green onions from the refrigerator, and you've got the makings of a quick–and feisty-flavored sauce.

SARDINE SAUCE

2 large garlic cloves, chopped
¼ cup olive oil
1 can (3.5 ounces) boneless sardines, drained
Grated zest of 1 medium lemon
2 tablespoons fresh lemon juice

Salt
Freshly ground black pepper
1 large green onion (green part only), chopped
½ cup fresh flat-leaf parsley, chopped

STIR GARLIC, oil, sardines, breaking them up into small pieces, lemon zest, lemon juice, salt, pepper, green onion, and parsley in large serving bowl. Add drained hot pasta and toss until combined. Serves 2 to 4.

Recommended Pasta: ½ pound penne rigate

TUNA, LEMON, AND CAPER SAUCE

1 large garlic clove, finely
    chopped
6.5-ounce can chunk light
    or solid white tuna,
    drained
Grated zest of 1 medium
    lemon
2 tablespoons fresh
    lemon juice
¼ cup olive oil

Salt
Freshly ground black
    pepper
2 tablespoons large capers,
    drained
¼ cup fresh flat-leaf parsley,
    chopped
Freshly grated Parmesan
    cheese

STIR GARLIC, tuna, breaking it up into bite-size pieces, lemon zest, lemon juice, olive oil, salt, pepper, capers, and parsley in large serving bowl. Add drained hot pasta and toss until combined. Serve with cheese if desired and pass the peppermill. Serves 2 to 4.

Recommended Pasta: ½ pound penne rigate

ne of the simplest and tastiest tuna sauces I know. ♦ For best results, purchase canned tuna (not flaked) that is packed in olive oil, although you may substitute tuna in water if preferred.

I just had to include this recipe from my book *Joie Warner's Spaghetti*. *I'd never encountered a smoked salmon pasta sauce that didn't contain heavy cream, so I created this light-and-elegant blend that's exceedingly simple, yet ever-so sophisticated.*

SMOKED SALMON, CAPERS, AND DILL SAUCE

6 ounces thinly sliced
 smoked salmon, very
 coarsely chopped
¼ cup plus 2 tablespoons
 olive oil
2 large garlic cloves, finely
 chopped
1 generous tablespoon
 tiny capers, drained

¼ cup coarsely chopped
 fresh dill
Freshly ground black
 pepper
2 tablespoons freshly
 grated Parmesan cheese,
 plus extra for serving
¼ cup diced red onion

PLACE SMOKED SALMON – separating pieces that clump together – in large serving bowl. Gently stir in oil, garlic, capers, dill, pepper, and cheese. Add drained hot pasta and toss until combined. Sprinkle with onion and serve with extra cheese. Serves 3 to 4.

Recommended Pasta: ½ pound spaghetti

SUN-DRIED TOMATO AND BLACK PEPPER SAUCE

1 cup sun-dried tomatoes
  in oil, well drained, diced
2 tablespoons olive oil
2 tablespoons sun-dried
  tomato oil
1 to 2 teaspoons cracked
  black pepper

¼ cup fresh basil leaves,
  coarsely chopped, plus
  extra for garnish
2 tablespoons freshly
  grated Parmesan cheese,
  plus extra for serving

PLACE SUN-DRIED TOMATOES, olive oil and sun-dried-tomato oil, cracked black pepper to taste, basil, and cheese in large serving bowl. Add drained hot pasta and toss until combined. Garnish with basil and serve with extra cheese. Serves 2 to 4.

Recommended Pasta: ½ pound spaghetti or fusilli

Sweet sun-dried tomatoes have a natural affinity for spicy cracked pepper. ◆ A pleasing impromptu pasta dinner from the pantry shelf.

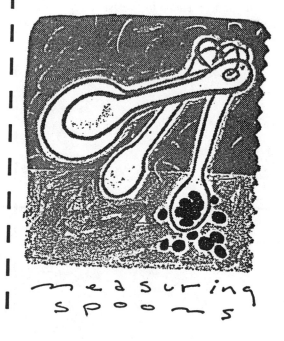

measuring spoons

Very intensely flavored, this sauce is based on the French black olive paste – tapenade.
♦ Don't be tempted to chop the ingredients in the food processor: the traditional recipe calls for chopping by hand and it's by far the best method.
♦ Grated orange zest and a small handful of shredded fresh basil may be added for more color and zip.

BLACK OLIVE PESTO SAUCE

2 large garlic cloves, chopped
¾ cup Greek black olives (Kalamata), pitted, chopped
¼ cup olive oil

Salt
Freshly ground black pepper
Freshly grated Parmesan cheese

PLACE CHOPPED GARLIC and olives in large serving bowl. Stir in oil, salt, and pepper. Add drained hot pasta and toss until combined. Serve with cheese if desired and pass the peppermill. Serves 4.

Recommended Pasta: ½ pound fusilli

TOMATO

SAUCES

♦ ♦ ♦

A romatic curry gives pasta a forceful flavor and bite. ◆ Excellent curry powder is essential. I purchase quality curry powder quite inexpensively in bulk at East-Indian food shops.

CURRIED TOMATO SAUCE

2 tablespoons olive oil
2 large garlic cloves, chopped
1 small onion, chopped
1 tablespoon best-quality curry powder
1 pound ripe cherry tomatoes, quartered

1 tablespoon butter
Salt
Freshly ground black pepper
Freshly grated Parmesan cheese

HEAT OIL in large nonstick skillet over medium-high heat. Add garlic and onion and cook for 2 minutes or until tender. Stir in curry powder and cook for several seconds or until fragrant. Add tomatoes, butter, salt, and pepper; cook for 2 minutes or just until cooked through. Add drained hot pasta to pan and toss until combined. Serve with cheese if desired. Serves 2 to 4.

Recommended Pasta: ½ pound penne rigate

GINGERY TOMATO SAUCE

2 tablespoons olive oil
2 large garlic cloves,
    chopped
1 tablespoon finely
    chopped fresh ginger
¼ teaspoon hot red pepper
    flakes
1 pound ripe cherry
    tomatoes, quartered

Salt
Freshly ground black
    pepper
¼ cup fresh cilantro leaves,
    chopped
2 tablespoons freshly
    grated Parmesan cheese,
    plus extra for serving

HEAT OIL in large nonstick skillet over medium-high heat. Add garlic, ginger, and red pepper flakes; cook for 1 minute or until tender. Add tomatoes, salt, and pepper; cook for 2 minutes or just until tomatoes are cooked through. Add drained hot pasta to pan and toss until combined. Sprinkle with cilantro and cheese; toss again. Serve with extra cheese. Serves 2 to 3.

Recommended Pasta: ½ pound penne rigate

E*ffortless to prepare and gingery hot: be sure to use fresh and flavorful ginger and tomatoes. ♦ If your tomatoes aren't ripe when you purchase them, leave them at room temperature until ripened. I never refrigerate tomatoes: chilling destroys the flavor.*

P iquant jalapeño-seasoned tomato sauce should be as hot and spicy as you can stand it – increase the amount of chiles at your peril!

TOMATO, JALAPEÑO, AND CILANTRO SAUCE

1 tablespoon olive oil
4 large garlic cloves, chopped
28-ounce can tomatoes, undrained
2 teaspoons dried oregano
Salt
Freshly ground black pepper

½ cup pickled sliced jalapeños, drained, coarsely chopped
½ cup fresh cilantro leaves, chopped, plus extra for garnish
Freshly grated Parmesan cheese

HEAT OIL in large nonstick skillet over medium-high heat. Add garlic and cook for 1 minute or until tender. Add tomatoes, crushing them with wooden spoon, oregano, salt, pepper, chiles, and cilantro; cook for 15 minutes or until slightly thickened. Add drained hot pasta to pan and toss until combined. Garnish with cilantro and serve with cheese. Serves 2 to 4.

Recommended Pasta: ½ pound penne rigate

TOMATO AND HORSERADISH SAUCE

1 tablespoon olive oil
4 large garlic cloves, chopped
1 medium onion, chopped
28-ounce can tomatoes, undrained
2 tablespoons extra-hot horseradish, drained
1 shot vodka

1 teaspoon dried basil
1 teaspoon Tabasco sauce
Salt
Freshly ground black pepper
Grated zest of 1 small lime (optional)
Freshly grated Parmesan cheese

HEAT OIL in large nonstick skillet over medium-high heat. Add garlic and onion and cook for 2 minutes or until tender. Add tomatoes, crushing them with wooden spoon, horseradish, vodka, basil, Tabasco, salt, and pepper; cook for 15 minutes or until slightly thickened. Add drained hot pasta to pan and toss until combined. Sprinkle with lime zest if desired and serve with cheese. Serves 4.

Recommended Pasta: ¾ pound spaghetti or linguine

My favorite cocktail – a Bloody Mary – inspired me to add horseradish and a shot of vodka to tomato sauce: they impart a subtle, yet toothsome, sharpness. ◆ *No Worcestershire sauce, please.*

Puttanesca sauce – that ever-so sprightly concoction, purportedly created by the "ladies-of-the-evening," is comprised of tomatoes, capers, and black olives. ♦ I've added a mix of sun-dried tomatoes, pancetta, and black and green olives, for a sauce that's even more gutsy and complex. ♦ The olives are unpitted, by the way, so do alert your dinner companions.

PUTTANESCA SAUCE WITH BLACK AND GREEN OLIVES

1 tablespoon olive oil
4 ounces thinly sliced pancetta, coarsely chopped
4 large garlic cloves, chopped
½ teaspoon hot red pepper flakes, or to taste
28-ounce can tomatoes, undrained
½ cup sun-dried tomatoes in oil, drained, diced

¼ cup French dry white vermouth
Freshly ground black pepper
1 generous tablespoon capers, drained
¾ cup Greek black olives (Kalamata), unpitted
½ cup green olives, unpitted
Freshly grated Parmesan cheese

HEAT OIL in large nonstick skillet over medium-high heat. Add pancetta and cook for 3 minutes or just until beginning to crisp. Add garlic and red pepper flakes and cook for 1 minute or until tender. Stir in tomatoes, crushing them with wooden spoon, sun-dried tomatoes, vermouth, and pepper. Cook for 15 minutes or until slightly thickened. Stir in capers and black and green olives. Add drained hot pasta to pan and toss until combined. Serve with cheese if desired. Serves 4.

Recommended Pasta: ½ pound penne rigate or rigatoni

SIMPLE TOMATO SAUCE

1 tablespoon olive oil
6 large garlic cloves,
  chopped
28-ounce can tomatoes,
  undrained
1 teaspoon sugar
1 teaspoon dried basil

2 teaspoons Tabasco
Salt
Freshly ground black
  pepper
Freshly grated Parmesan
  cheese

HEAT OIL in large nonstick skillet over medium-high heat. Add garlic and cook for 1 minute or until tender. Add tomatoes, crushing them with wooden spoon, sugar, basil, Tabasco, salt, and pepper; cook for 15 minutes or until slightly thickened. Add drained hot pasta to pan and toss until combined. Serve with cheese. Serves 4.

Recommended Pasta: ¾ pound spaghetti, linguine, or vermicelli

Simple and appealing, the "secret" ingredient is the Tabasco sauce. Don't be tempted to leave it out: it adds spirited flavor and plenty of heat.

canned tomatoes

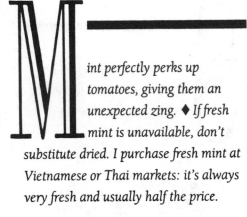

int perfectly perks up tomatoes, giving them an unexpected zing. ♦ If fresh mint is unavailable, don't substitute dried. I purchase fresh mint at Vietnamese or Thai markets: it's always very fresh and usually half the price.

MINTY TOMATO SAUCE

1 tablespoon olive oil
4 large garlic cloves, chopped
28-ounce can tomatoes, undrained
Salt
Freshly ground black pepper

¼ to ½ cup fresh mint leaves, coarsely chopped
¼ cup (½ stick) butter
¼ cup freshly grated Parmesan cheese, plus extra for serving

HEAT OIL in large nonstick skillet over medium-high heat. Add garlic and cook for 1 minute or until tender. Add tomatoes, crushing them with wooden spoon, salt, and pepper; cook for 15 minutes or until slightly thickened. Just before serving, stir in mint (some mint is stronger flavored than others, so taste as you go), butter, and cheese. Add drained hot pasta to pan and toss until combined. (It may seem as if there is too much sauce, but extra-thin pasta absorbs sauce on standing.) Serve with extra cheese. Serves 2 to 3.

Recommended Pasta: ½ pound vermicelli

TOMATO AND MARINATED ARTICHOKE SAUCE

1 tablespoon olive oil
6 large garlic cloves, chopped
2 tablespoons bottled hot pepper rings, drained, chopped
28-ounce can tomatoes, undrained, puréed in food processor
2 tablespoons French dry white vermouth
1 teaspoon dried basil
Salt

Freshly ground black pepper
2 jars (6-ounces each) marinated artichoke hearts, drained, coarsely chopped
½ cup Greek black olives (Kalamata), unpitted or pitted
½ cup fresh flat-leaf parsley, chopped
Freshly grated Parmesan cheese

HEAT OIL in large nonstick skillet over medium-high heat. Add garlic and cook for 1 minute or until tender. Add hot peppers, puréed tomatoes, vermouth, basil, salt, and pepper and cook for 15 minutes or until slightly thickened. Stir in artichoke hearts, olives, and parsley. Add drained hot pasta to pan and toss until combined. Serve with cheese. Serves 2 to 4.

Recommended Pasta: ½ pound penne rigate or fusilli

M arinated artichoke hearts are an unbeatable addition to tomato sauce. ♦ The pow of pickled hot peppers and the punch of black olives add a special spice and tang.

Millions of variations have been devised for marinara sauce. My favorite version features a marvelous mingling of mushrooms and tomatoes for a result that is seriously superb.

MUSHROOM MARINARA SAUCE

1 tablespoon olive oil
6 large garlic cloves, chopped
1 medium onion, chopped
¼ teaspoon hot red pepper flakes
1 pound fresh mushrooms, thinly sliced
28-ounce can tomatoes, undrained, puréed in food processor
1 teaspoon sugar

1 teaspoon dried oregano
1 teaspoon dried basil
½ cup fresh flat-leaf parsley, chopped
Salt
Freshly ground black pepper
¼ cup (½ stick) butter
2 tablespoons freshly grated Romano or Parmesan cheese, plus extra for serving

HEAT OIL in large nonstick skillet over medium-high heat. Add garlic, onion, and red pepper flakes; cook for 2 minutes or until tender. Add mushrooms and cook for 3 minutes or just until beginning to brown. Stir in puréed tomatoes, sugar, oregano, basil, parsley, salt, and pepper; cook for 15 minutes or until slightly thickened. Stir in butter and cheese. Add drained hot pasta to pan and toss until combined. Serve with extra cheese and pass the peppermill. Serves 2 to 4.

Recommended Pasta: ½ pound penne rigate

TOMATO AND RED CHILE PEPPER SAUCE

2 tablespoons olive oil	Salt
2 large garlic cloves, chopped	Freshly ground black pepper
1 teaspoon hot red pepper flakes	Freshly grated Parmesan cheese
1 pound ripe cherry tomatoes, quartered	
8 large sun-dried tomato halves in oil, drained, diced	

HEAT OIL in large nonstick skillet over medium-high heat. Add garlic and red pepper flakes; cook for 1 minute or until tender. Add tomatoes, sun-dried tomatoes, salt, and pepper; cook for 2 minutes or just until tomatoes are cooked through. Add drained hot pasta to pan and toss until combined. Serve with cheese if desired. Serves 2 to 3.

Recommended Pasta: ½ pound penne rigate

C*alled Arrabiata in Italian, which translates into "enraged," you can probably guess that this sauce is very hot. It's also extraordinarily good.*

Laced with fresh basil and the hint of lemon and balsamic vinegar, this tomato sauce is tangier than most. ◆ It's imperative to cook tomato sauce in a nonreactive pan – one that won't react with acid foods. I use a nonstick skillet, but because of the extra acids – lemon and vinegar – don't use a pan with even a slightly damaged nonstick surface, or the sauce could have a bitter metallic taste.

BASIL TOMATO SAUCE

1 tablespoon olive oil
4 large garlic cloves, chopped
1 medium-small onion, chopped
28-ounce can tomatoes, undrained
1 cup fresh basil leaves, chopped
1 teaspoon dried basil
Grated zest of 1 medium lemon
2 teaspoons sugar
Salt
1 tablespoon best-quality balsamic vinegar (no substitute)
Freshly grated Parmesan cheese

HEAT OIL in large nonstick skillet over medium-high heat. Add garlic and onion and cook for 2 minutes or until tender. Add tomatoes, crushing them with wooden spoon, fresh basil, dried basil, lemon zest, sugar, and salt; cook for 15 minutes or until slightly thickened. Turn off heat and stir in balsamic vinegar. Add drained hot pasta to pan and toss until combined. Serve with cheese. Serves 4.

Recommended Pasta: ½ pound penne rigate

TOMATO SAUCE WITH MELTED MOZZARELLA

1 tablespoon olive oil
4 large garlic cloves, chopped
¼ teaspoon hot red pepper flakes
28-ounce can tomatoes, undrained
1 teaspoon dried oregano
Salt

Freshly ground black pepper
½ cup fresh basil leaves, chopped
8 ounces mozzarella cheese, very coarsely grated
Freshly grated Parmesan cheese

HEAT OIL in large nonstick skillet over medium-high heat. Add garlic and red pepper flakes and cook for 1 minute or until tender. Add tomatoes, crushing them with wooden spoon, oregano, salt, and pepper and cook for 15 minutes or until slightly thickened. Add drained hot pasta to pan and toss until combined. Sprinkle with basil and mozzarella cheese and toss again until cheese is melted. Serve at once with Parmesan cheese. Serves 4.

Recommended Pasta: ½ pound penne rigate or fusilli

*S*atisfying indeed! Here, pasta is swathed in a simple tomato sauce with melted mozzarella. Monterey Jack or Italian (not domestic) Fontina cheese may be substituted for mozzarella.

G orgonzola may seem an unlikely soul mate for tomato sauce, but I guarantee you'll find the combination creates a blissful blending of flavors with a very special lushness.

CREAMY TOMATO AND GORGONZOLA SAUCE

¼ cup (½ stick) butter
4 large garlic cloves, chopped
28-ounce can tomatoes, undrained
½ cup fresh basil leaves, chopped

Salt
Freshly ground black pepper
8 ounces Gorgonzola cheese, crumbled
Freshly grated Parmesan cheese

MELT BUTTER in large nonstick skillet over medium-high heat. Add garlic and cook for 1 minute or until tender. Add tomatoes, crushing them with wooden spoon, then stir in half the basil, salt, and pepper. Simmer for 15 minutes or until slightly thickened. Reduce heat to low, add Gorgonzola, and stir until thoroughly blended. Add drained hot pasta to pan, sprinkle with remaining basil, and toss until combined. (It may seem as if there is too much sauce, but it thickens on standing.) Serve with Parmesan cheese and pass the peppermill. Serves 2 to 4.

Recommended Pasta: ½ pound penne rigate or rigatoni

CHEESE & BUTTER

SAUCES

◆ ◆ ◆

My mother often likes to tease me – the pasta cookbook author – about my old fondness for "instant" macaroni and cheese. So, for fun one day, I decided to try to recreate the pasta of my childhood. Those were the days before I discovered that pasta – a.k.a. macaroni – didn't come in a box with packets of powdered sauce! ◆ There's still millions of kids who love instant macaroni and cheese, so why not make it from scratch? ◆ To jazz it up for grown-ups, garnish with some diced sun-dried tomatoes and a sprinkling of cayenne.

INSTANT CHEESE SAUCE

¼ cup plus 2 tablespoons butter
¼ cup plus 2 tablespoons milk
¼ cup plus 2 tablespoons freshly grated Romano cheese (not Parmesan)

¼ cup plus 2 tablespoons nonfat dry milk

MELT BUTTER in heavy medium saucepan over medium heat. Add milk and bring to a boil. Remove from heat and add cheese and dry milk. Return to heat and stir a few seconds or until slightly thickened. Add drained hot pasta to pan and stir until combined. (If you prefer more sauce, add a little more milk, cheese, and dry milk and stir until heated through.) Serves 2 to 4.

Recommended Pasta: 1½ cups small elbow macaroni or conchigliette (little shells)

CREAMY BLUE CHEESE SAUCE

2 tablespoons butter
2 large garlic cloves,
   chopped
1 cup half-and-half
8 ounces Gorgonzola
   cheese, crumbled
Salt
Lots of freshly ground
   black pepper

Grated zest of 1 medium
   lemon
2 tablespoons fresh
   lemon juice
¼ cup freshly grated
   Parmesan cheese

MELT BUTTER in large nonstick skillet over medium-high heat. Add garlic and cook for 1 minute or until tender. Add half-and-half, Gorgonzola cheese, salt, and pepper; cook, whisking until smooth, for 4 minutes or until slightly thickened. Stir in lemon zest, lemon juice, and Parmesan cheese. Add drained hot pasta to pan and toss until combined. (It may seem as if there is too much sauce, but it thickens on standing.) Serves 4.

Recommended Pasta: ½ pound penne rigate, rigatoni, macaroni, or spaghetti

A somewhat lighter – yet still luscious – version of blue cheese sauce, made with half-and-half instead of heavy cream. ♦ It's still quite rich, so be sure to serve a simple green salad as an accompaniment.

citrus juicer

5 1

Cooking butter until nicely browned and nutty flavored, then adding finely grated mezithra cheese is a classic, richly flavored, Greek spaghetti sauce. ◆ Mezithra is available at Greek and specialty cheese shops. If unavailable, substitute freshly grated Romano.

BROWNED BUTTER SAUCE

¼ cup (½ stick) butter
¼ cup freshly grated mezithra or Romano cheese
Freshly ground black pepper

2 green onions (green part only), chopped
Unflavored yogurt or sour cream (optional)

MELT BUTTER in large nonstick skillet over medium-high heat for 3 minutes, or until it begins to brown – watch carefully so that it doesn't burn. Immediately remove from heat. Add drained hot pasta to pan and toss until combined. Sprinkle with cheese, pepper, and green onions; toss again. Serve with a dollop of yogurt or sour cream if desired. Serves 4.

Recommended Pasta: ½ pound penne rigate or spaghetti

t doesn't get much simpler than this!

BROWNED BUTTER AND SAGE SAUCE

¼ cup (½ stick) butter
2 tablespoons chopped
fresh sage leaves
(not dried)

Freshly grated Parmesan
cheese

MELT BUTTER in large nonstick skillet over medium-high heat. Add sage and cook for 3 minutes or until butter begins to brown and sage becomes crispy – watch carefully so that butter doesn't burn. Immediately remove from heat. Add drained hot pasta to pan and toss until combined. Serve with cheese. Serves 2 to 4.

Recommended Pasta: ½ pound fusilli, penne rigate, cheese ravioli, or tortellini

J ust when you think there's nothing left to eat in the pantry, consider this frugal Italian classic – invented during the War when cheese was very expensive. ♦ *Freshly-made breadcrumbs are essential.* ♦ *To make breadcrumbs: use* good *Italian or French bread (including crusts) and either chop by hand or in a food processor – not super fine.*

TOASTED BREADCRUMB SAUCE

¼ cup olive oil
1 cup freshly-made
  breadcrumbs
4 large garlic cloves,
  chopped
¼ cup fresh flat-leaf parsley,
  finely chopped

Salt
Freshly ground black
  pepper
Freshly grated Parmesan
  cheese

HEAT OIL in large nonstick skillet over medium-high heat. Add breadcrumbs and cook for 4 minutes or until crisp and golden. Add garlic and cook for 30 seconds or until tender. Add drained hot pasta to pan, sprinkle with parsley, salt, and pepper and toss until combined. Serve with cheese. Serves 2 to 4.

Recommended Pasta: ½ pound spaghetti or linguine

VEGETABLE & BEAN

SAUCES

◆ ◆ ◆

Yellow and red peppers are swiftly sautéed with tangy capers and fragrant basil. ♦ If yellow peppers are unavailable, substitute another red – not green – pepper. A truly enchanting and pretty entrée when tossed with fusilli or farfalle.

SWEET RED AND YELLOW PEPPER SAUCE

¼ cup olive oil
2 large garlic cloves, finely chopped
¼ teaspoon hot red pepper flakes
1 medium-small sweet red pepper, seeded, diced
1 medium-small sweet yellow pepper, seeded, diced

2 tablespoons tiny capers, drained
Salt
Freshly ground black pepper
2 tablespoons freshly grated Parmesan cheese, plus extra for serving
½ cup fresh basil leaves, coarsely shredded

HEAT OIL in large nonstick skillet over medium-high heat. Add garlic, red pepper flakes, and red and yellow peppers and cook for 2 minutes or just until peppers are tender; do not overcook. Add drained hot pasta to pan, sprinkle with capers, salt, pepper, cheese, and basil and toss for several seconds for pasta to absorb flavors. Serve with extra cheese and pass the peppermill. Serves 2 to 4.

Recommended Pasta: ½ pound farfalle

THREE PEPPER SAUCE

¼ cup olive oil
2 large garlic cloves, chopped
1 medium-small onion, chopped
1 medium sweet red pepper, seeded, diced
½ teaspoon dried basil
6-ounce jar roasted red peppers, drained, coarsely chopped

2 tablespoons bottled hot pepper rings, drained, coarsely chopped
Salt
Freshly ground black pepper
½ cup fresh basil leaves, chopped
Freshly grated Parmesan cheese

HEAT OIL in large nonstick skillet over medium high-heat. Add garlic, onion, sweet red pepper, and dried basil; cook for 2 minutes or until tender. Add roasted red peppers, hot pepper rings, salt, and pepper; cook for 1 minute or until heated through. Add drained hot pasta to pan, sprinkle with basil, and toss until combined. Serve with cheese. Serves 2 to 4.

Recommended Pasta: ½ pound penne rigate or fusilli

Vivid in both color and taste — fresh red peppers are sautéed with roasted red peppers and pickled hot pepper rings to create a ravishing sauce with just a bit of bite.

H ave jars of roasted red peppers, marinated artichokes, and capers handy? Just toss in a few Kalamata olives and you can whip up the flavors of the Mediterranean in a flash. ♦ I'm especially fond of this exuberant blend.

ARTICHOKE, RED PEPPER, AND OLIVE SAUCE

1 tablespoon olive oil
4 large garlic cloves, chopped
1 medium-small onion, chopped
¼ teaspoon hot red pepper flakes
6-ounce jar marinated artichoke hearts, drained, reserving marinade, coarsely chopped
6-ounce jar roasted red peppers, drained, coarsely chopped

10 Greek black olives (Kalamata), pitted, cut into strips
½ teaspoon dried basil
Salt
Freshly ground black pepper
Freshly grated Parmesan cheese

HEAT OIL in large nonstick skillet over medium-high heat. Add garlic, onion, and red pepper flakes; cook for 2 minutes or until tender. Add artichoke hearts and reserved marinade, red peppers, olives, basil, salt, and pepper; cook for 2 minutes or until heated through. Add drained hot pasta to pan and toss until combined. Serve with cheese if desired and pass the peppermill. Serves 2 to 4.

Recommended Pasta: ½ pound penne rigate or rigatoni

ROASTED SWEET RED PEPPER SAUCE

1 tablespoon butter
1 tablespoon olive oil
3 large garlic cloves, chopped
1 cup chopped red onion
3 medium sweet red peppers, roasted, peeled, seeded, chopped
1 ⅓ cups chicken stock

Salt
Freshly ground black pepper
½ cup fresh basil leaves, chopped
Grated zest of 1 medium lemon
Freshly grated Parmesan cheese

MELT BUTTER with oil in large nonstick skillet over medium-high heat. Add garlic and onion and cook for 2 minutes or until tender. Add peppers, chicken stock, salt, and pepper and simmer for 10 minutes. Purée in food processor and return to pan. Simmer mixture for 4 minutes or until slightly thickened. Add drained hot pasta to pan, sprinkle with basil and lemon zest, and toss until combined. Serve with cheese. Serves 4.

Recommended Pasta: ¾ pound spaghetti

Beguiling roasted red peppers bewitched by fresh basil and the zing of lemon zest bring you a very special pasta sauce. ♦ A speedier – and still sensational – alternative is to eliminate the roasting process. Simply seed and chop the red peppers, then cook with the garlic and onion just until tender.

itrus and cilantro perk up a simple, and simply satisfying, mushroom sauce.

CITRUSY MUSHROOM SAUCE

¼ cup olive oil
2 large garlic cloves, chopped
1 scant tablespoon dried oregano
⅛ teaspoon cayenne
1 pound fresh mushrooms, coarsely chopped
Grated zest of 1 medium lemon

Grated zest of 1 medium-large orange
Salt
Freshly ground black pepper
½ cup fresh cilantro leaves, coarsely chopped
¼ cup freshly grated Parmesan cheese

HEAT OIL in large nonstick skillet over medium-high heat. Add garlic, oregano, and cayenne; cook for 1 minute or until tender. Add mushrooms, lemon and orange zests, and cook for 2 minutes or just until mushrooms are beginning to brown. Sprinkle with salt and pepper. Add drained hot pasta to pan, sprinkle with cilantro and cheese, and toss until combined. Serves 2 to 4.

Recommended Pasta: ½ pound spaghetti or linguine

mushrooms

CREMINI MUSHROOM AND FRESH MINT SAUCE

1 tablespoon olive oil
4 large garlic cloves, chopped
1 pound fresh brown mushrooms (cremini), coarsely chopped
¼ cup chicken stock
¼ cup French dry white vermouth
¼ cup fresh mint leaves, chopped
1 tablespoon butter
Salt
Freshly ground black pepper
2 tablespoons freshly grated Parmesan cheese, plus extra for serving

HEAT OIL in large nonstick skillet over medium-high heat. Add garlic and mushrooms and cook for 4 minutes. Add stock and cook for a few seconds; add vermouth and continue cooking for a few minutes more or until about ¼ cup liquid remains. (Some mushrooms exude more liquid than others. If too much liquid remains after 4 minutes, drain off all but ¼ cup.) Add drained hot pasta to pan, sprinkle with mint, and add butter, salt, pepper, and cheese. Toss for 1 minute or until pasta absorbs some of the liquid. Serve with extra cheese. Serves 2 to 4.

Recommended Pasta: ½ pound spaghetti or linguine

Fresh mint with mushrooms is a commonly found combination in the south of Italy. ♦ I love mushrooms and a favorite variation of this recipe is to substitute a medley of "exotic" mushrooms (½ pound oyster, ¼ pound shiitake, and ¼ pound chanterelles or cremini mushrooms), omitting the mint.

Warning! For garlic devotees only! A gratifying – and very garlicky – variation on the classic garlic-and-oil theme. Here, a – need I say – copious amount of garlic is braised in chicken stock until it becomes rich and caramelized.

BRAISED GARLIC SAUCE

26 large garlic cloves, peeled, left whole
1 cup chicken stock
1 teaspoon plus ¼ cup olive oil
¼ teaspoon hot red pepper flakes
Salt

Freshly ground black pepper
1 cup fresh flat-leaf parsley, chopped
¼ cup freshly grated Romano or Parmesan cheese, plus extra for serving

PLACE GARLIC, chicken stock, and 1 teaspoon oil in large nonstick skillet; bring to a boil over medium-high heat. Reduce heat to medium and simmer, uncovered, for 15 to 20 minutes or until garlic is tender and caramelized and just a little liquid remains. Add scant ¼ cup oil, red pepper flakes, salt, and pepper; cook for 1 minute or until heated through. Add drained hot pasta to pan, sprinkle with parsley and cheese, and toss until combined. Serve with extra cheese. Serves 2 to 4.

Recommended Pasta: ½ pound spaghetti or linguine

GARLIC AND POTATO SAUCE

3 large potatoes (1½
  pounds), peeled or
  unpeeled, cubed
⅓ cup olive oil
Salt
Freshly ground black
  pepper
10 large garlic cloves,
  coarsely chopped

¼ teaspoon hot red
  pepper flakes
½ cup fresh flat-leaf
  parsley, coarsely
  chopped
Freshly grated Parmesan
  cheese

DROP POTATOES into saucepan of boiling water and cook for 8 minutes or just until tender; drain well.

Heat oil in large nonstick skillet over medium-high heat. Add potatoes, salt, and pepper; cook for 10 minutes or until crisp and golden. Reduce heat to medium-low; add garlic and red pepper flakes and cook for 1 minute or until tender. Add drained hot pasta to pan, sprinkle with parsley, and toss until combined. Taste and add more salt if necessary and serve with cheese. Serves 2 to 4.

Recommended Pasta: ½ pound spaghetti or linguine

P *leasantly peasanty – with potatoes, garlic, red pepper flakes, and parsley – this is one of those pasta sauces whose ordinary-sounding ingredients can fool you. Try it! You just might get a tasty surprise!*

Roasting vegetables in the oven gives them a gorgeous grilled flavor and appearance – their looks and taste make heavenly harmonies with pasta. ♦ I use an inexpensive but heavy, shiny black nonstick low-sided baking sheet (about 10 x 15 inches) for oven grilling. ♦ Bright aluminum pans inhibit darkening; black pans encourage browning.

OVEN-GRILLED VEGETABLE SAUCE

4 large garlic cloves, chopped
1 large sweet red pepper, seeded, cut into ½- x 1-inch pieces
1 large sweet yellow pepper, seeded, cut into ½- x 1-inch pieces
2 Japanese eggplants, unpeeled, halved lengthwise, sliced crosswise into ½-inch thick pieces

1 small red onion, cut into 1-inch pieces
1 cup fresh basil leaves, chopped
⅓ cup plus 1 tablespoon olive oil
¼ cup freshly grated Parmesan cheese, plus extra for serving
Salt
Freshly ground black pepper

PREHEAT OVEN to 450°F; adjust oven rack to highest shelf.
Combine garlic, red and yellow peppers, eggplants, onion, ½ cup basil, ⅓ cup oil, and cheese in large bowl. Spread vegetable mixture on large, low-sided (or vegetables will steam), heavy nonstick baking sheet. Bake for 30 minutes or until vegetables are tender and edges have charred here and there. Transfer mixture to large serving bowl, add drained hot pasta, and toss until combined. Sprinkle with remaining basil, salt, pepper, and remaining oil, if mixture seems dry; toss again. Serve with extra cheese and pass the peppermill. Serves 4.

Recommended Pasta: ½ pound penne rigate, rigatoni, gnocchi, fusilli, or conchiglie

Oven-Grilled Asparagus, Red Pepper, and Mushroom Sauce

1 pound fresh asparagus, tough ends snapped off, discarded
2 large sweet red peppers, seeded, cut into ½- x 2-inch pieces
4 large garlic cloves, chopped
1 small red onion, cut into 1-inch pieces
8 medium-large cremini mushrooms, halved

1 teaspoon dried oregano
Freshly ground black pepper
⅓ cup olive oil
¼ cup freshly grated Parmesan cheese, plus extra for serving
Salt
½ cup fresh basil leaves, chopped

PREHEAT OVEN to 450°F; adjust oven rack to highest shelf.

Combine asparagus, red peppers, garlic, onion, mushrooms, oregano, pepper, oil, and cheese in large bowl. Spread vegetable mixture on large (about 10 x 15 inches), low-sided (or vegetables will steam), heavy black nonstick baking sheet. Bake for 20 to 30 minutes or until vegetables are tender and edges have charred here and there. Transfer mixture to large serving bowl, add drained hot pasta, salt, and basil; toss until combined. Serve with extra cheese and pass the peppermill. Serves 4.

Recommended Pasta: ½ pound penne rigate or fusilli

A carnival of vegetables – slender asparagus, sweet red peppers, and mushrooms – are oven-grilled for an intense smoky flavor.

eggplant is briefly broiled, then tossed with garlic, fragrant fresh basil, crunchy pecans, and enlivened with a splash of vinegar. The resulting sauce is especially piquant and utterly delectable tossed with any cup-shaped pasta to catch the pieces of eggplant. ◆ When buying eggplant, be sure to select only those that seem heavy for their size, with smooth, shiny, taut, and unblemished skin.

EGGPLANT, BASIL, AND TOASTED PECAN SAUCE

2 large eggplants (1 pound each), unpeeled, sliced into ½-inch thick rounds
Salt
¼ cup olive oil
1 large garlic clove, chopped
½ teaspoon hot red pepper flakes, or to taste
½ cup fresh basil leaves, chopped
¼ cup pecan halves, toasted, chopped (not too fine)
2 tablespoons red wine vinegar
Freshly grated Parmesan cheese

SPRINKLE EGGPLANT SLICES on both sides with salt and place in 2 large colanders; set aside for 45 minutes to drain, then thoroughly pat dry with paper towels.

Preheat broiler.

Brush both sides of eggplant slices lightly with some of the oil, then place on large nonstick baking sheet or broiling rack (or do in batches). Broil for 3 to 4 minutes each side or just until cooked through and nicely browned in spots. When cool enough to handle, cut into 1-inch cubes; set aside.

Heat remaining oil in large nonstick skillet over medium-high heat. Add garlic and red pepper flakes and cook for 1 minute or until tender. Add eggplant, basil, and half the pecans; sprinkle with vinegar and toss until combined. Add drained hot pasta to pan and toss again. Garnish each serving with remaining pecans. Serve with cheese if desired and pass the peppermill. Serves 4.

Recommended Pasta: ½ pound gnocchi, conchiglie, or penne rigate

LIMA BEAN AND BACON SAUCE

6 ounces thinly sliced
  pancetta, coarsely
  chopped
¼ cup olive oil
4 large garlic cloves,
  chopped
¼ teaspoon hot red pepper
  flakes
14 ounces fresh or frozen
  baby lima beans, cooked

¾ pound cherry tomatoes,
  quartered
1½ teaspoons dried thyme
Salt
Freshly ground black
  pepper
¼ cup freshly grated
  Romano cheese, plus
  extra for serving

COOK PANCETTA in large nonstick skillet over medium-high heat for 3 minutes or until just beginning to crisp. Remove to plate; set aside.

Add oil; when hot, add garlic and red pepper flakes and cook for 1 minute or until tender. Add beans, tomatoes, thyme, salt, and pepper; cook for 2 minutes or just until heated through. Add drained hot pasta to pan and toss until combined. Sprinkle with cheese; toss again. Top with pancetta and serve with extra cheese. Serves 2 to 4.

Recommended Pasta: ½ pound penne rigate

Lima beans belong to that family of foods you either like or dislike intensely. I happen to think they're super so, taking my cue from the French, I combined their distinctive character with bacon – well, Italian bacon actually – pancetta. Do go ahead and give them a try – these just might be the best lima beans you've ever eaten.

G enoa sausage imparts a peppery piquancy to cannellini beans and tomatoes. ◆ This rugged pasta makes a splendid supper dish.

WHITE BEAN, TOMATO, AND GENOA SAUSAGE SAUCE

1 tablespoon olive oil
4 large garlic cloves, chopped
¼ teaspoon hot red pepper flakes
28-ounce can tomatoes, undrained
6 ounces thinly sliced Genoa sausage, coarsely chopped

19-ounce can cannellini (white kidney) beans, drained, rinsed
1 teaspoon dried basil
Salt
2 tablespoons butter
¾ cup fresh flat-leaf parsley, chopped
Freshly grated Parmesan cheese

HEAT OIL in large nonstick skillet over medium-high heat. Add garlic and red pepper flakes and cook for 1 minute or until tender. Add tomatoes, crushing them with wooden spoon, Genoa sausage, beans, basil, and salt. Cook for 15 minutes or until slightly thickened; stir in butter. Add drained hot pasta to pan, sprinkle with parsley, and toss until combined. Serve with cheese. Serves 4.

Recommended Pasta: ½ pound penne rigate, rigatoni, fusilli, or ziti

CHICKPEA AND ESCAROLE SAUCE

1 tablespoon olive oil
1 large garlic clove,
  chopped
¼ teaspoon hot red pepper
  flakes
1 head escarole, well
  washed, green leaves cut
  into wide shreds

½ cup chicken stock
19-ounce can chickpeas,
  drained
Salt
Freshly ground black
  pepper
Freshly grated Parmesan
  cheese

HEAT OIL in large nonstick skillet over medium-high heat. Add garlic and red pepper flakes and cook for 1 minute or until tender. Add escarole and toss for 2 minutes or just until wilted. Stir in chicken stock, chickpeas, salt, and pepper; cook for 2 minutes or until heated through. Add pasta and toss for 1 minute to absorb some of the liquid and flavor. Serve with cheese if desired. Serves 2 to 4.

Recommended Pasta: ½ pound orecchiette, penne rigate, or gnocchi

N*utritious and delicious, who could ask for anything more?* ◆ *Add only a pinch of red pepper flakes if you're the least bit heat-shy: some find the sauce hot even with only ¼ teaspoon red pepper flakes.* ◆ *Serve in wide shallow pasta bowls as the sauce is slightly soupy.*

Not long ago, someone wrote anonymously to me and vaguely described a pasta sauce containing peas and onions. Why it was sent I'll never know. I can only guess they wanted me to create a recipe. So I hope this simple, homey dish is what they were after!

GREEN PEA, PROSCIUTTO, AND ONION SAUCE

1 tablespoon olive oil	Salt
2 large garlic cloves, chopped	Freshly ground black pepper
1 cup chopped sweet white onion	6 ounces thinly sliced prosciutto, cut into ¼-inch strips
⅓ cup chicken stock	Freshly grated Parmesan cheese
1½ cups fresh or frozen tiny peas	
2 to 3 tablespoons butter	

HEAT OIL in large nonstick skillet over medium-high heat. Add garlic and onion; cook for 2 minutes or until tender. Add stock and bring to a boil. Add peas and cook for several seconds or just until heated through. Stir in butter, salt, and pepper. Add drained hot pasta to pan, add prosciutto, and toss until combined. Serve with cheese. Serves 2 to 4.

Recommended Pasta: ½ pound fusilli, orecchiette, conchiglie, or gnocchi

SEAFOOD & FISH

SAUCES

◆ ◆ ◆

Fabulously fetching. Sweet shrimp and ripe tomatoes are fragrant with fresh and dried herbs. ♦ This glorious sauce – from my spaghetti cookbook – is perfect for a special dinner.

SHRIMP, FRESH TOMATO, AND HERB SAUCE

¼ cup olive oil
4 large garlic cloves, chopped
½ teaspoon hot red pepper flakes
1 teaspoon dried oregano
1 teaspoon dried basil
1 pound raw medium shrimp, peeled, deveined
¾ pound ripe cherry tomatoes, quartered
Salt

Freshly ground black pepper
¼ cup freshly grated Parmesan cheese, plus extra for serving
¼ cup fresh flat-leaf parsley, chopped
¼ cup fresh basil leaves, chopped
Grated zest of 1 medium lemon

HEAT OIL in large nonstick skillet over medium-high heat. Add garlic, red pepper flakes, oregano, dried basil, and shrimp; cook for 2 minutes or just until shrimp are opaque. Add tomatoes, salt, and pepper and cook for 2 minutes or just until tomatoes are cooked through. Add drained hot pasta to pan and toss until combined. Sprinkle with cheese, parsley, basil, and lemon zest; toss again. Serve with extra cheese. Serves 2 to 4.

Recommended Pasta: ½ pound spaghetti

SEAFOOD TOMATO SAUCE

1 tablespoon olive oil
4 large garlic cloves, chopped
1 medium-small onion, chopped
½ teaspoon hot red pepper flakes, or to taste
28-ounce can tomatoes, undrained, puréed in food processor
1 teaspoon dried basil
1 teaspoon dried oregano

Salt
Freshly ground black pepper
1 pound raw medium shrimp, peeled, deveined
¼ cup fresh flat-leaf parsley, chopped
1 tablespoon butter
2 tablespoons freshly grated Parmesan cheese, plus extra for serving

*U*se truly sweet-smelling shrimp, purchased from a quality fish store, and you will be richly rewarded.
♦ *I like to toss this sauce with conchiglie – seafood with seashells, of course – but it's perfectly delightful with other pasta shapes, too.*

HEAT OIL in large nonstick skillet over medium-high heat. Add garlic, onion, and red pepper flakes; cook for 2 minutes or until tender. Add puréed tomatoes, basil, oregano, salt, and pepper; cook for 15 minutes or until slightly thickened. Reduce heat, add shrimp, and cook for 2 minutes or until opaque – do not overcook. Stir in parsley and butter. Add drained hot pasta to pan, sprinkle with cheese, and toss until combined. Serve with extra cheese if desired. Serves 4.

Recommended Pasta: ½ pound conchiglie, gnocchi, or penne rigate

shrimp

By now you've probably noticed I'm addicted to olives – not to mention garlic and lemons! – and I use them generously to jazz up lots and lots of dishes. Here, their pungency is a perfect contrast to the sweet shrimp.

SHRIMP AND BLACK OLIVE SAUCE

¼ cup olive oil
Grated zest of 1 large lemon
2 large garlic cloves, chopped
½ teaspoon hot red pepper flakes, or to taste
1 pound raw medium shrimp, peeled, deveined
2 tablespoons fresh lemon juice

½ cup Greek black olives (Kalamata), pitted, cut into strips
1 teaspoon dried oregano
½ cup fresh flat-leaf parsley, chopped
Freshly grated Parmesan cheese

HEAT OIL in large nonstick skillet over medium-high heat. Add lemon zest, garlic, red pepper flakes, and shrimp; cook for 2 minutes or just until shrimp are opaque. Stir in lemon juice, olives, oregano, and parsley. Add drained hot pasta to pan and toss until combined. Serve with cheese if desired. Serves 2 to 4.

Recommended Pasta: ½ pound penne rigate

SHRIMP, FETA, AND TOMATO SAUCE

¼ cup olive oil
2 large garlic cloves, chopped
1 teaspoon dried oregano
½ teaspoon hot red pepper flakes, or to taste
1 pound raw medium shrimp, peeled, deveined
¾ pound ripe cherry tomatoes, quartered

Salt
Freshly ground black pepper
1 cup crumbled feta cheese
2 large green onions (green part only), chopped
Freshly grated Parmesan cheese

*G*reek influences – shrimp, tomatoes, oregano, and feta cheese – echo in this remarkably robust pasta sauce.

HEAT OIL in large nonstick skillet over medium-high heat. Add garlic, oregano, red pepper flakes, and shrimp; cook for 2 minutes or just until shrimp are opaque. Add tomatoes, salt, and pepper and cook for 2 minutes or just until tomatoes are cooked through. Add drained hot pasta to pan and toss until combined. Sprinkle with feta and green onions; toss again. Serve with Parmesan cheese if desired. Serves 4.

Recommended Pasta: ½ pound penne rigate

Crab – here reminiscent of Louisiana – is captivating with the spicy bite of cayenne and hot sauce. ◆ Fresh lump crabmeat is best, frozen will do, but imitation crab is just not on.

HOT AND SPICY CRAB SAUCE

1 tablespoon olive oil
1 large garlic clove,
   chopped
3 tablespoons butter
2 teaspoons Tabasco

⅛ teaspoon cayenne
8 ounces crabmeat, if
   frozen, thawed, squeezed
   dry, picked over

HEAT OIL in large nonstick skillet over medium-high heat. Add garlic and cook for 1 minute or until tender. Add 2 tablespoons butter, Tabasco, and cayenne, stirring until blended. Stir in crab and cook, breaking up meat into bite-size pieces, for 1 minute or just until heated through – do not overcook. Add drained hot pasta to pan and remaining butter and toss until combined. Serve at once. Serves 2.

Recommended Pasta: ¼ pound penne rigate

SCALLOPS AND TOASTED BREADCRUMB SAUCE

¼ cup olive oil
1 cup fresh breadcrumbs
2 large garlic cloves, chopped
¼ teaspoon hot red pepper flakes
½ pound fresh bay or sea scallops, patted dry, coarsely diced

Salt
Freshly ground black pepper
¼ cup fresh flat-leaf parsley, chopped

HEAT 2 TABLESPOONS OIL in large nonstick skillet over medium-high heat. Add breadcrumbs and cook for 4 minutes or until crisp and golden. Transfer crumbs to plate; set aside.

Add remaining oil, garlic, red pepper flakes, scallops, salt, and pepper; cook for several seconds or just until scallops are opaque – do not overcook. Add drained hot pasta to pan and toss until combined. Sprinkle with breadcrumbs and parsley; toss again. Serves 2 to 3.

Recommended Pasta: ½ pound spaghettini or vermicelli

This is an adaptation of a recipe from Marcella Hazan's More Classic Italian Cooking. Freshly-made breadcrumbs – not too fine – are essential – make them from good Italian or French bread. Never use scallops that are frozen, or that have ever been frozen.

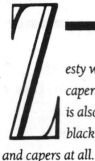

esty with stuffed green olives, capers, and lemon, the sauce is also pleasing with Greek black olives, or with no olives and capers at all.

TUNA, TOMATO, AND GREEN OLIVE SAUCE

1 tablespoon olive oil
4 large garlic cloves, chopped
¼ teaspoon hot red pepper flakes
28-ounce can tomatoes, undrained
Salt
Freshly ground black pepper
7-ounce can chunk light or solid white tuna (not flaked), drained

½ cup pimento-stuffed green olives, coarsely chopped
1 tablespoon large capers, drained
1 tablespoon butter
Grated zest of 1 small lemon
¼ cup fresh flat-leaf parsley, chopped
Freshly grated Parmesan cheese

HEAT OIL in large nonstick skillet over medium-high heat. Add garlic and red pepper flakes and cook for 1 minute or until tender. Add tomatoes, crushing them with wooden spoon, salt, and pepper; cook for 15 minutes or until slightly thickened. Stir in tuna, breaking it into bite-size pieces, olives, capers, butter, lemon zest, and parsley. Add drained hot pasta to pan and toss until combined. Serve with cheese if desired. Serves 4.

Recommended Pasta: ½ pound penne rigate, fusilli, or rigatoni

GARLIC AND CLAM SAUCE

1 tablespoon olive oil
1 large carrot, diced
8 large garlic cloves,
    chopped
2 cans (5 ounces each)
    baby clams, drained,
    reserving ¼ cup broth
¼ cup French dry white
    vermouth

1 teaspoon dried basil
Salt
Freshly ground black
    pepper
2 to 3 tablespoons butter
1 cup fresh flat-leaf parsley,
    chopped
Freshly grated Parmesan
    cheese

HEAT OIL in large nonstick skillet over medium-high heat. Add carrot and cook for 3 minutes or just until tender. Add garlic and cook for 1 minute. Add reserved clam broth, vermouth, basil, salt, and pepper; bring to a boil. Cook for several minutes or until liquid is reduced by half. Stir in butter and clams. Add drained hot pasta to pan, sprinkle with parsley, and toss for 1 minute or until pasta absorbs some of the liquid. Serve with cheese if desired and pass the peppermill. Serves 3 to 4.

Recommended Pasta: ½ pound linguine or spaghetti

When fresh clams are not available, you can still serve up a speedy seafood sauce. Try this garlicky version prepared with canned clams – and carrots for color and crunch. ♦ Because the sauce is somewhat soupy, serve it in wide shallow pasta bowls.

cheese
grater

MEAT

SAUCES

◆ ◆ ◆

Half-and-half cream combined with tomatoes creates a characteristic rich and creamy, pink-hued sauce that's highlighted by the addition of tiny, bright-green peas.

CREAMY TOMATO AND SAUSAGE SAUCE

1 tablespoon olive oil
4 large garlic cloves, chopped
¼ teaspoon hot red pepper flakes
1 pound sweet Italian sausage, casings removed
28-ounce can tomatoes, undrained, puréed in food processor
1 tablespoon dried oregano
½ cup half-and-half
Salt
Freshly ground black pepper
¾ cup frozen green peas, thawed
¼ cup freshly grated Parmesan cheese, plus extra for serving

HEAT OIL in large nonstick skillet over medium-high heat. Add garlic and hot red pepper flakes and cook for 1 minute or until tender. Add sausage and cook, breaking up meat with fork, until no pink remains. Tilt pan and discard excess oil. Add puréed tomatoes, oregano, half-and-half, salt, and pepper; cook for 15 minutes or until slightly thickened. Just before serving, stir in peas and cheese. Add drained hot pasta to pan and toss until combined. Serve with extra cheese. Serves 4.

Recommended Pasta: ½ pound penne rigate, rigatoni, fusilli, or gnocchi

BROCCOLI AND ITALIAN SAUSAGE SAUCE

2 tablespoons olive oil
1 pound sweet or hot Italian sausage, cut into ½-inch thick slices
4 large garlic cloves, chopped
¼ teaspoon hot red pepper flakes
3 cups coarsely chopped broccoli florets (no thick stems)

Salt
Freshly ground black pepper
2 tablespoons water
¼ cup freshly grated Parmesan or Romano cheese, plus extra for serving

HEAT OIL in large nonstick skillet over medium-high heat. Add sausage and cook for 10 minutes or until no pink remains. Add garlic, red pepper flakes, broccoli, salt, and pepper; cook for 1 minute or until garlic is tender. Add 2 tablespoons water; immediately turn heat to high, cover, and steam for 2 minutes or just until broccoli is brilliant green and crisp-tender. Add drained hot pasta to pan, sprinkle with cheese, and toss until combined. Serve with extra cheese. Serves 2 to 4.

Recommended Pasta: ½ pound penne rigate or rigatoni

B*rimming with brilliant-green broccoli and sweet or spicy Italian sausage, this sauce deserves a gutsy red wine and a basket of country bread. ◆ Excellent Italian sausage is essential.*

uick and simple – a handy, dandy standby.

QUICK MEAT SAUCE

1 tablespoon olive oil
4 large garlic cloves, chopped
¼ teaspoon hot red pepper flakes
1 medium onion, chopped
¾ pound ground beef or pork
28-ounce can tomatoes, undrained, puréed in food processor

2 teaspoons dried oregano
Salt
Freshly ground black pepper
¼ teaspoon ground cinnamon
½ cup freshly grated Parmesan cheese, plus extra for serving

HEAT OIL in large nonstick skillet over medium-high heat. Add garlic, red pepper flakes, and onion; cook for 2 minutes or until tender. Add beef and cook, breaking up meat with fork, until no pink remains. Tilt pan and discard excess oil. Add puréed tomatoes, oregano, salt, pepper, cinnamon, and half the cheese; cook for 15 minutes or until slightly thickened. Stir in remaining cheese. Add drained hot pasta to pan and toss until combined. Serve with extra cheese if desired. Serves 4.

Recommended Pasta: ½ pound penne rigate or rigatoni

BOLOGNESE SAUCE

1 tablespoon olive oil
1 large garlic clove,
    chopped
¾ cup chopped fresh
    fennel bulb
1 medium carrot, diced
1 small onion, chopped
4 ounces thinly sliced
    pancetta, coarsely
    chopped
¾ pound ground beef or
    pork, or a combination
    of both
28-ounce can tomatoes,
    undrained, puréed in
    food processor

1 teaspoon dried basil
1 teaspoon dried oregano
¼ cup French dry white
    vermouth
¼ cup chicken stock
Salt
Freshly ground black
    pepper
2 tablespoons butter
Freshly grated Parmesan
    cheese

Classic meaty ragu takes hours to cook, but not this wonderful quick-and-easy version. Long-cooking simply tenderizes the meat (not really necessary in this day and age), but, if you want to be truly authentic, simmer the sauce very gently for an hour or more.

HEAT OIL in large nonstick skillet over medium-high heat. Add garlic, fennel, carrot, onion, and pancetta; cook for 4 minutes or until vegetables are tender. Add beef and cook, breaking up meat with fork, until no pink remains. Tilt pan and discard excess oil. Stir in puréed tomatoes, basil, oregano, vermouth, chicken stock, salt, and pepper; cook for 20 minutes or until slightly thickened. Stir in butter. Add drained hot pasta to pan and toss until combined. Serve with cheese. Serves 4 to 6.

Recommended Pasta: ¾ to 1 pound penne rigate, rigatoni, fusilli, or spaghetti

Tex-Mex chili – prepared with lean ground beef, a generous jolt of jalapeños, and the very best chili powder you can find – is very hot: adjust seasonings to taste. ♦ Serve accompanied by bowls of grated Monterey Jack or Cheddar cheese, sour cream, and chopped cilantro for guests to add to their liking.

BEEF CHILI SAUCE

1 tablespoon olive oil
1 medium onion, chopped
4 large garlic cloves, chopped
¾ pound lean ground beef
28-ounce can tomatoes, undrained, puréed in food processor
¼ cup pickled sliced jalapeños, drained, coarsely chopped

2 tablespoons best-quality chili powder
1 tablespoon dried oregano
Salt
⅛ teaspoon ground cloves
Grated Monterey Jack or Cheddar cheese
Sour cream
Fresh cilantro leaves, coarsely chopped

HEAT OIL in large nonstick skillet over medium-high heat. Add onion and garlic and cook for 2 minutes or until tender. Add beef and cook, breaking up meat with fork, until no pink remains. Tilt pan and discard excess oil. Stir in puréed tomatoes, chiles, chili powder, oregano, salt, and cloves; cook for 10 minutes or until slightly thickened. Add drained hot pasta to pan and toss until combined. Serve with separate bowls of cheese, sour cream, and cilantro. Serves 4.

Recommended Pasta: ½ pound penne rigate or rigatoni

HEARTY TOMATO SAUCE WITH ITALIAN SAUSAGE

2 tablespoons olive oil
1 pound pork spareribs, cut into ribs
2 pounds sweet Italian sausage, cut into ½-thick slices
12 large garlic cloves, chopped
2 cans (28 ounces each) tomatoes, undrained, puréed in food processor
5½-ounce can tomato paste
2 tablespoons dried basil
1 teaspoon hot red pepper flakes, or to taste
6-inch cinnamon stick
1½ teaspoons fennel seeds
Grated zest of 1 medium lemon
Salt
Freshly ground black pepper
Freshly grated Romano or Parmesan cheese

Prepare to enjoy this roundly sustaining, extra-hot-and-spicy, spareribs-and-sausage sauce. It really is the sort of homey fare everyone appreciates. ◆ The sauce is only as good as the sausage, so be sure to use only the best.

HEAT OIL in very large nonstick skillet over medium-high heat. Brown spareribs and sausages in batches and transfer to plate; drain and discard all but 1 teaspoon oil. (If you don't have a pan large enough to hold both meat and sauce, brown the meat in a large skillet, then transfer to a large, heavy, nonreactive saucepan.) Add garlic and cook for 1 minute or until tender. Stir in puréed tomatoes, tomato paste, basil, red pepper flakes, cinnamon, fennel seeds, lemon zest, salt, and pepper. Return meat, bring to a boil, then reduce heat and simmer for 45 minutes or until meat is tender and sauce slightly thickened. Remove ribs to separate serving dish and discard cinnamon stick. Add drained hot pasta to pan and toss until combined. Serve with cheese. Serves 8.

Recommended Pasta: 1½ pounds spaghetti or linguine

Styled after a hearty sauce from the region of Amatrice, just northeast of Rome, I've combined tomatoes with sun-dried tomatoes, onions, and pancetta for a distinctive sauce with unforgettable flavor. ◆ Pancetta is an unsmoked Italian bacon, cured in salt, that is available in many supermarkets and Italian food stores. Don't substitute bacon; it imparts a smoky flavor.

TOMATO, PANCETTA, AND ONION SAUCE

1 tablespoon olive oil
6 ounces thinly sliced pancetta, cut into ½-inch pieces
2 large garlic cloves, chopped
1 medium onion, chopped
¼ teaspoon hot red pepper flakes
28-ounce can tomatoes, undrained
½ cup sun-dried tomatoes in oil, drained, diced
¼ cup French dry white vermouth
Salt
Freshly ground black pepper
Freshly grated Parmesan cheese

HEAT OIL in large nonstick skillet over medium-high heat. Add pancetta, garlic, onion, and red pepper flakes; cook for 2 minutes or until onion is tender. Add tomatoes, crushing them with wooden spoon, sun-dried tomatoes, vermouth, salt, and pepper and cook for 15 minutes or until slightly thickened. Add drained hot pasta to pan and toss until combined. Serve with cheese. Serves 4.

Recommended Pasta: ½ pound gnocchi, penne rigate, or fusilli

PROSCIUTTO AND BLACK PEPPER SAUCE

1 tablespoon olive oil
2 large garlic cloves, chopped
2 tablespoons butter
Grated zest of 1 large lemon
6 ounces thinly sliced prosciutto, cut into ¼-inch strips

1½ teaspoons cracked black pepper
2 tablespoons freshly grated Parmesan cheese, plus extra for serving

HEAT OIL in large nonstick skillet over medium-high heat. Add garlic and cook for 1 minute or until tender. Remove from heat, stir in butter and lemon zest. Add drained hot pasta to pan and toss until combined. Add prosciutto, pepper, and cheese; toss until combined. Serve with extra cheese. Serves 2 to 4.

Recommended Pasta: ½ pound vermicelli or capellini

S alty prosciutto is balanced by the zest of lemon and the pizzazz of plenty of black pepper. A good choice for any of the thin-cut pastas.

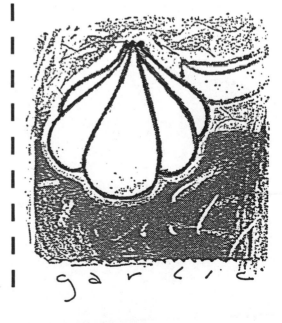
garlic

INDEX

◆ ◆ ◆

INDEX

◆ ◆ ◆

Books in Joie Warner's ALL THE BEST series

Available from
HEARST/WILLIAM MORROW

Books in Joie Warner's ALL THE BEST series

also available

Available from
HEARST/WILLIAM MORROW